As far as Hilary Duff is concerned, she's just like any other teenager. "I hang out, do chores, do homework, and occasionally get grounded," she explains.

Just your average teen, right?

Well, not exactly. No matter how normal she tries to be, Hilary Duff is a superstar. With her movie and television career booming and her music career white-hot, Hilary would be hard-pressed to fade into the background.

That kind of fame could change a girl—but it hasn't spoiled Hilary. She's still the sweet girl she's always been. This is your chance to meet the *real* Hilary Duff!

hilary duff
a not-so-typical teen

NANCY KRULIK

SIMON SPOTLIGHT™

New York London Toronto Sydney Singapore

For Sarah and Emily

This book is neither authorized nor endorsed by Hilary Duff or any of the production companies listed herein.

First Simon Spotlight edition September 2003

Text copyright © 2003 by Nancy Krulik

Simon Spotlight
An imprint of Simon & Schuster
Children's Publishing Division
1230 Avenue of the Americas
New York, NY 10020

SIMON SPOTLIGHT is a trademark of Simon & Schuster.

Designed by Ann Sullivan
The text of this book was set in Berkeley.

Printed in the United States of America
10 9

Library of Congress Control Number 2003108564
ISBN 0-689-86781-6

Table of Contents

1. | "I Think I'm a Regular Kid"

As far as Hilary Duff is concerned, she's just like any other teenager. "You know something, I think I'm a regular kid," she told one chat audience. "I hang out, do chores, do homework, and occasionally get grounded."

On the surface it sure looks like Hilary's a typical teen. Consider what she was up to during the spring and summer of 2003—when she was fifteen years old. Most of the time Hilary was busy with the usual teen activities. She never went anywhere without her cell phone in her purse, and she worried about looking bad in photographs. The biggest thing in her life was prepping for her driving test. "I can get my learner's permit now," she told *Popstar!* magazine. And she was already hoping that when she turned sixteen, her parents would buy her a car. After all, they'd bought her big sister Haylie a set of wheels when she turned sixteen. So of course Hil was expecting the same.

The summer of 2003 also found Hilary in the throes of planning a blow-out sweet sixteen party for herself. As she told *E! Online*, "For the past couple of years . . . my birthdays haven't meant that much to me. I've gone out with friends and stuff; [for my sweet 16] I'm going all out."

Like other teenagers, Hilary spends a lot of time at the mall. She admits to having a control issue when it comes to shopping. "I love clothes. I have a huge fetish for shoes, clothes, and makeup," she told one fan magazine. "I'm the kind of person who doesn't like to wear things over and over again." Is it any wonder then that her favorite fantasy is a "mall day when I could go to every store and pick out everything I wanted"?

Part of that fashion passion stems from the fact that, like many fifteen-year-olds, in the summer of 2003 Hilary had begun to date. And looking good for the guys was a top priority. Although she was more likely to head out for a night on the town with a crowd than on a one-on-one car date, she still had her eye on a few lucky guys. And she wanted to dress in a way that would get her noticed, yet was still flattering.

See, *normal teen behavior.*

Dating often leads to kissing. In 2003, Hilary admitted to a chat audience that she'd kissed a boy or two recently. (Although she said she hoped "my mom and dad don't read this.")

At times Hilary's dating life has been cut short by her being grounded. Like just about every other teenage girl in the world, Hilary and her mom don't always see eye-to-eye (although they are extremely close). Superstar or not, Hilary's mom isn't about to let Hilary misbehave. Hilary admits that although being grounded stinks, she has done things to deserve it. And when given time to think about her actions, her conscience usually kicks in, and she feels bad about her behavior.

Hil told *Girls' Life* magazine that one of her worst memories was of a fight she had with her mom. "I said something mean to my mom because I was grounded for not taking care of my room. I felt so bad about it. It took me a while to do the right thing and apologize for saying something hurtful—when I was really mad at myself for not taking care of business."

So Hilary's just your average teen, right?

Well, not exactly. Let's face it, no matter how normal she tries to be, Hilary Duff is a superstar. *Lizzie McGuire*, the TV show in which she plays the title character, is the number one TV show on the Disney Channel. *The Lizzie McGuire Movie* came in number two at the box office in its opening weekend in May 2003, following only the mega-huge *X2: X-Men United*. And at the same time, her pop single, "Why Not?" was moving up the charts on MTV's viewer-voting phenomenon, *TRL*.

Sorry Hilary, it's not possible to fade into the teenage crowd when you've got all that going on.

In fact, at closer look, Hilary Duff is anything but normal. Consider her dating situation—she wasn't just going out with the guy next door. Hilary's first serious boyfriend was none other than pop sensation (and Backstreet Boy little bro) Aaron Carter. And they didn't just go to the movies. They went to the premiere of Hilary's film, *The Lizzie McGuire Movie*.

As for all that kissing, that wasn't always your typical romantic scenario either. In fact, Hilary's first kiss was on the set of her TV show, *Lizzie McGuire*. It was anything but romantic. Imagine having to smooch a guy with cameramen, castmates, lighting and prop people, your school tutor, the makeup artists, hair stylists, and a director all staring at you.

"It was awkward," Hilary admitted to *TV Guide*. "They were all making fun of me and I was like, 'I can't wait for this to be over.'"

To top it all off, unlike her TV alter ego, Hilary

doesn't even really go to school. She's tutored on the set. "My life is a lot different (from Lizzie's)," she explained to *TV Guide*, "because I don't go to middle school and I don't really go through some of the problems Lizzie goes through."

Not that Hilary doesn't have problems of her own. Her on-again, off-again romance with Aaron Carter has made headline news (at the moment they're off again because Hilary couldn't handle Aaron's "player" ways), and it's tough for her to go to the mall or the movies without being swamped by fans. Her busy schedule leaves little time for just chillin', and while other teens are prepping for parties and proms, Hilary's jetting across the country doing publicity for her album or her acting career.

That could be a lot for a teen to handle. Even the usually sunny Hilary has admitted that not every day is great. "I have bad days like everyone else," she told *Popstar!* magazine. "But I keep them in perspective and just wait for the sun to shine again."

For now those bad days seem few and far between. Hilary Duff is blessed with a great family and close friends, both in Los Angeles and in her home state of Texas. Her music career is white-hot, and when it comes to acting, there isn't a teenager in America who's more loved than she is.

That kind of fame could change a girl. But it hasn't

changed Hilary. She's still the sweet girl she's always been. She worries, though, that people might not see that. "Sometimes people might think 'oh, look at her,' or assume I'm bratty," she told *Blast!* magazine. "I wish they knew what I was really like."

This is your chance to make Hilary's wish come true. Meet the real Hilary Duff.

| 2. | A Star Is Born! |

Hilary Ann Duff was born on September 28, 1987. Her parents, Bob and Susan Duff, brought their pink bundle home to an already kid-friendly house. Hilary's older sister, Haylie, was two and a half when Hil arrived, and by all accounts the big sis was thrilled to have someone even smaller than she in the family.

From day one Hilary worshipped Haylie. As soon as Hil's little hazel eyes could focus, they followed Haylie around the room. It was Haylie who brought the biggest smiles to Hilary's chubby face, and it was Haylie who first brought out Hilary's famous giggle.

Hilary admits that Haylie has always been her role model. She told *TRL* that although she loves the styles J Lo and Britney Spears put together, she gets most of her style tips from Haylie. Since day one, she's the one Hilary has most aspired to be like.

From the time the Duff girls were very little, they would perform around the house, putting on shows for their parents and for each other. Eventually Haylie added a little professionalism to her home performances by taking ballet lessons.

Hilary should have taken on the nickname "Me Too," because that was exactly what she demanded when she saw her older sister putting on a leotard and ballet slippers and going off to class. When she was six, Hilary followed in Haylie's dancing footsteps and began dance lessons.

Hilary's admiration of her big sister is actually very typical. Psychologists who study the effects of birth order in a family have figured out that younger children are often very influenced by their big sibs. The older kids try to teach the younger ones the things they've learned in the big world. And the younger kids just idolize their older brothers and sisters.

Eventually though, younger siblings do break out on their own. It just takes them a while. But when they do, younger kids like Hil are often the most outgoing, creative, and funny people in the family.

When Hilary started dancing just like Haylie, she loved it. (Hey, what little girl doesn't love ballet class, right?) Lots of kids dream of being ballerinas when they grow up. But the naturally impatient Hilary wasn't planning on waiting that long. From the very first class, Hilary decided dancing was what she wanted to do. Her teachers agreed that Hilary just might have had what it took to be a professional dancer. Soon she joined big sis, Haylie, performing with some local ballet companies. It wasn't long before Hilary found herself making her stage debut—as a child in Texas's BalletMet Columbus production of *The Nutcracker*.

The Duff girls spent several years performing pirouettes. But eventually Haylie's interest turned elsewhere. According to Hilary, "My sister was doing a *Romeo and Juliet* Shakespeare play and she didn't want be bad in front of her friends. So there was a little acting workshop near our house, and she started to go."

After enrolling Haylie in acting lessons, Susan Duff found herself being pulled in two directions— taking Haylie to acting classes and dropping Hilary off at the dance studio.

For a while everything settled into a routine. Hilary was happy dancing while Haylie pursued her acting. As Hilary told a chat audience, "When I was a little girl I didn't think (acting) was what I wanted to do." But then Hilary's severe case of big sister worship returned. Hilary wanted to stop dancing and start acting.

"My older sister actually wanted to be an actress and singer. She kept coming home showing me all this stuff she was doing [in acting class] and I was, 'Mom, I want to do that,'" Hilary recalled to *TeenHollywood.com*. "So I just kind of followed in her footsteps."

Hilary can be awfully persuasive when she wants to be (who could ever say no to those big, innocent hazel eyes, right?), and before anyone knew what was happening, Susan Duff was running around Texas, bringing both her daughters to auditions for local theater projects and commercials.

From the very start Hilary knew she was meant to act. For the little girl, acting was magic—a chance to pretend and play dress up, and get applause for it. In Hil's case, that magical feeling has never gone away. "I love being an actress," she admitted to a chat audience. "It's great to put myself in someone else's shoes and then go home and be myself."

The girls had some limited success in the Houston area. Haylie was the first to land a small role, in the TV-movie *Hope*, which was directed by Goldie Hawn and filmed in Texas. Hilary managed to score her first local commercial when she was about seven years old. A few months later she earned a role in a TV movie called *True Women* that was filming in Texas.

True Women was a quality story. The TV film, which starred Rachel Leigh Cook and Tina Majornio, told the tale of two best friends who are separated when they're teenagers, but manage to keep their friendship alive. Hilary's part in *True Women* was so small her name never even appeared in the credits. It wasn't exactly a star-making turn. Still Hilary was proud to be in the movie. And somehow, she instinctively knew that next time she'd get a part that was big enough to earn her the credit she deserved.

But let's face it, Houston is not the movie capital of the world. If Hilary and Haylie were really going to pursue stardom, they'd have to make a big move—halfway across the country.

"We talked my mom into taking us to California," Hilary told a Disney Records chat audience. "Then we started going on many auditions."

The move to California was not without problems. For starters, only Susan Duff and the girls moved out there. Bob Duff remained in Houston, where he's a partner in a chain of convenience stores. Bob made the trip to California every three weeks (a schedule he still keeps up today) to visit with his wife and daughters.

That wasn't the only big change to the girls' lives.

Although the girls liked the more temperate climate ("I don't live [in Houston] anymore, so I don't sweat as much," Hilary has been known to say), the professional life in California was a shocker. Haylie and Hil were overwhelmed by the sudden surge in competition. In Houston there were a limited number of kid actors auditioning for the same roles. But Los Angeles is filled with adorable child performers, all vying for the same few parts.

Susan Duff wasn't going to let a little stiff competition get in the way of her girls' dreams. If they wanted to be actresses she would support them any way she could—and that meant being on the other end of a lot of frustrating telephone hang-ups.

"When we first came out here, we were here a month, and [my mom] rented an apartment for us and she got all these books about the business," Hilary told *TeenHollywood.com*. "She would call people up and go, 'I have these two really cute girls from Texas,' and it was like, *click*. It was so hard, but she did it."

Susan Duff's hard work paid off in 1997, when both Haylie and Hilary managed to get parts in direct-to-video films. Haylie won the role of Gina Adams, a cousin of the creepy, kooky Addams family in *An Addams Family Reunion*. It was a small role, but a role just the same. Getting cast in a Hollywood film gave her a lot of confidence.

It wasn't long before Haylie's little sis got some work of her own. Ironically, Hilary's movie dealt with some hilarious haunted folks as well. It was called *Casper Meets Wendy*, and was another exciting adventure in the lives of Wendy and her pal Casper the Friendly Ghost.

When she was cast as Wendy in the movie, Hilary began work on her very first starring role. *Casper Meets Wendy* was a comedy with a strong message: Just because someone looks different it does not mean they are less of a person (or ghost, for that matter).

Hilary had a blast working on the film. Although it was her first experience with special effects, Hilary loved all the action and running around that playing the role of Wendy demanded.

Some of that action caused her a lot of embarrassment. To this day she recalls one really bizarre experience on the set. "On the set of my first movie, *Casper Meets Wendy*, I was chasing a goat for this one scene," she told *Girls' Life* magazine. "The director kept screaming 'Meaner! Meaner!' I ran faster with this really angry expression on my face. The director yelled 'Cut! Hilary what are you doing?' I told him I was just following directions. Turns out he was calling the goat. His name was Meaner."

Hilary's acting with Meaner, Casper, and several

assorted witches grabbed the attention of the folks who do the nominating for the Young Artist Awards. Hil was nominated in the Best Leading Young Actress performance in a TV Movie Pilot/Miniseries or Series—Young Actress Age Ten or Under category for her work in *Casper Meets Wendy*. Although she didn't win, just being nominated was an extremely big deal for a girl so new to Hollywood.

It seemed as though the Duff girls were on their way. After all, they'd hardly been in California and already they were both working. But you can't take anything for granted in Hollywood, a fact which Haylie and Hilary both learned the hard way. When production ended on *The Addams Family Reunion* and *Casper Meets Wendy*, the girls went back to making audition rounds. It would be nearly two years before either of them would work again.

Hilary recalls that time in her life as being really frustrating. "It's almost like a craving or an addiction," Hilary told *Entertainment Weekly*. "You want to keep working."

Most kids would have given up long before that two year mark ever rolled around. But Hilary Duff is not most kids. She's a determined young lady who doesn't give up on her goals. So she just kept on auditioning, putting herself into her career heart and *soul*.

3. | The Soul of an Actress

In 1999 Hilary was cast in the role of Ellie in the made-for-TV movie *The Soul Collector*. Ellie was not a leading role, but it was a meaty supporting part. Hilary was just glad for the work.

The Soul Collector's main character was an angel named Zachariah, who makes quite a few heavenly errors and is sentenced to live on earth as a human for thirty days, helping some real humans make the transition between life and death.

It was a heavy subject for an eleven-year-old to tackle, but Hilary was able to pull off her part quite well. Best of all, the movie was filmed in Texas, which meant Hilary got to spend some time on her home turf during the shoot. That home-court advantage must have been good for Hil, because her work in the film was universally praised. By the end of 2000 Hilary had an award to her name. She was the winner of the Young Artists Award for Best Performance in a TV Movie or Pilot—Supporting Young Actress.

Hilary was on her way. Not long after winning the award, Hil got cast in a guest starring role in the medical TV drama *Chicago Hope*. She played a little girl named Jessie Seldon in an episode entitled "Cold Hearts."

The part in *Chicago Hope* was just one week's worth of work. But a few months later Hilary was presented with an opportunity to be a regular in a weekly series for NBC. She was cast as a daughter in the pilot for a new TV show called *Daddio*. Hil was thrilled to have gotten the part, even though she knew there were no guarantees *Daddio* would ever hit the airwaves.

Many TV shows begin as pilots—single episodes that are produced for network executives to view. If the network execs think that the show has a future, more episodes are ordered, and the show is given a chance with a real audience. Each year hundreds of pilots are shot, and only a few ever get on TV.

But *Daddio* had a shot. It starred actor Michael Chiklis in the title role. Michael was well known in TV circles, having starred in both *The Commish* and

St. Michael's Crossing as well as several well-reviewed feature films. (He later went on to earn a 2003 Emmy and a 2002 Golden Globe award for Best Actor in a drama for his performance in *The Shield*.) The producers were hoping Michael's fame would be enough to make the *Daddio* pilot stand out in a crowd. Their strategy worked. *Daddio* was picked up by NBC. The network announced it would begin airing episodes of the show as a mid season replacement in March 2000.

You would think news like that would have made Hilary happy. And it would have—had she not been cut from the final cast of the show. Although Hilary had been cast as one of the daughters in the pilot, the producers opted to replace her with another actress when they began to film the actual episodes of the show. Hilary was certain she'd lost her chance at TV stardom. She was devastated. The rejection almost caused her to end her career. "I was wanting to quit," she admitted to *Entertainment Weekly*.

It's a good thing she didn't. Just three weeks later Susan Duff got a call asking Hilary to audition for another show. It wasn't a broadcast network show, rather it was being prepared for the Disney Channel, a relatively new cable network (at least compared to NBC). The Disney folks were looking for an actress to play the title role in a show about kids in middle school. The role Hilary would be auditioning for would be a girl who wasn't particularly popular, athletic, or brainy. As Hilary described her on CBS's *The Early Show*, "She struggles through school, trying to fit in. She has embarrassing parents and an annoying little brother. She's just kind of insecure and she's trying to find herself."

In other words, she was just a typical teenager. Which, as you know, is exactly how Hilary has always thought of herself.

But as perfect as the part may have seemed for her, Hilary really didn't want to go on the audition. She was tired and fed up. As she explained to one chat audience, "I was thinking of taking a break because I was so disappointed about *Daddio*."

But after reading the script, both Susan and Hilary agreed that Hil would be perfect for the show. She absolutely had to audition for this one.

The original script for the show was called *What's Lizzie Thinking?* Eventually, the name of the show was changed to *Lizzie McGuire*. The rest, as they say, is history.

| 4. | Stepping into Lizzie's Shoes |

The *Lizzie McGuire* auditions were a grueling experience for Hilary. The producers had a lot riding on this series, and they needed just the right actress to play their title role. They wanted someone who stood out from the crowd—but who was still able to be the all-American every girl. It wasn't easy to find someone like that.

Until Hilary Duff walked into the room.

Hilary once told a chat audience that she thought it was possible that the producers of *Lizzie McGuire* picked her to play the title role because they liked the way she could stand on her head. "At the time, I loved my yo-yo and walking on my hands. I think they thought that was different," she explained.

Well, although Hilary's upside-down talents are

quite remarkable, the show's executive producer, Stan Rogow, tells a different tale.

"We were looking for an average girl," Stan told *Entertainment Weekly*. As he explained, the character of Lizzie was, "defined by what she wasn't. She wasn't the popular girl, she wasn't the diva, she wasn't the jock. She was just Lizzie."

It took several rounds of auditions for the *Lizzie McGuire* producers to decide on an actress to play their leading lady. Not only did Hil have to read lines with other actors, she had to prove that she could do voice-over work, for those moments when the script called for the animated Lizzie to speak.

Voice-over work may look easy, since all you have to do is talk into a microphone. But for many actors, it can be some of the toughest work they'll ever do. Actors, particularly film and TV actors, often depend on their facial expressions and body language to help them tell a story. In voice-over work, those are meaningless. The voice-over actor has to be able to convey emotions with just her voice.

Luckily that's something Hilary excels in. In fact, she loves voice-over work. Later, after she'd been doing the animated Lizzie's voice for a while, she told a chat audience that, "I have fun with animated Lizzie because she says what [Lizzie] is thinking but knows better than to say. It's so much fun matching my voice with [the animated] Lizzie's mouth."

Hilary could also match many of Lizzie's less-than-graceful actions. The actress admits that, like Lizzie, she can be a bit of klutz.

"I can do some pretty lame things," Hil admitted to a chat room. "Like rocking back and forth on the heels of my shoes and my feet fly right out from underneath me!"

Eventually the producers of *Lizzie McGuire* came to the right conclusion. Of all the girls who'd auditioned for the role, there was only one who had the looks, charm, talent, and klutzy cuteness to take on the part of Lizzie. And that girl was Hilary Duff.

Lizzie McGuire was Hilary's first regular role on a TV series. That brought a certain status in Hollywood. And in show biz, status is often reflected in salary. Although no one has officially said how much Hilary earned in the first years of the show, it was rumored that she earned about $15,000 per episode. That's not in that million-plus league like the cast of *Friends* earns per episode, but it's a lot more than chump change—especially for a teenager who was basically an unknown at the time. (Of course, Hilary doesn't get most of the money she earns right now. Like all child actors, most of it is put in a trust for her to use when she's an adult. That's why she has to do chores around the house and save up for the things she really wants, just like anybody else.)

Being a series regular meant that Hilary spent every day with the same people day in and day out. That's much different than movie work. In a movie you work closely with people for a few weeks, and then you go your separate ways. A TV series is more like a regular job. You really get to know your costars.

Hilary's costars were a lot like her—kids who'd just recently gotten started in the business without a huge amount of credit to their names. That was a calculated risk on the part of the producers. They wanted kids who would be natural on camera, not affected Hollywood-type kids. And they didn't want famous actors who were already associated with other characters. They wanted their audience to feel that the characters on TV were ordinary kids they could meet in their own school.

That's exactly what the producers got. Lalaine, an actress from Burbank, California, was cast as Lizzie's female best friend, Miranda. Before stepping onto the *Lizzie McGuire* set, Lalaine's claim to fame had been more theatrical. She'd played Cosette in a national touring company of *Les Miserables*, and Kate in the 1999 TV movie, *Annie*.

Adam Lamberg, the actor cast as Lizzie's other best pal, Gordo, has said he will never forget what it felt like to be cast in *Lizzie McGuire*. "They gave me a couple of scenes to read, and I read with Hilary," he told *TeenMag.com*. "I was pretty nervous. There were two other guys there, so I was sort of eyeing them, seeing whether or not they were better than me."

Luckily, Adam had something—or make that *two* things—that made him stand out from the crowd. "It was funny, because a couple of weeks before I had broken both my wrists, so I did the whole screen test with two casts on both my arms. I think that kind of made me stick out a little, and that may have helped me get the part." (Those soulful big eyes that just scream brainy and sexy didn't hurt either, Adam!)

Adam had slightly more experience than Hilary and Lalaine, having performed small roles in the miniseries *Dead Man's Walk*, the show *I'm Not Rappaport*, and the made-for-TV movie, *The Day Lincoln Was Shot*. He'd also had a role in the made-for-TV movie *Radiant City*, in which he played Kirstie Alley's son, Stewie. Unlike the girls, Adam was an East Coast kid—he was born in New York. His 1984 birthday also made him the oldest kid on the set.

All those differences did set him apart a bit. Although everyone got along great on the *Lizzie* set,

23

if pressed to tell the truth, Adam had to admit that he didn't really socialize with the other cast members when they weren't at work. "The girls are a little bit younger than me so I don't really hang out with them too much off the set," he told *Teenmag.com*.

The role of Lizzie's annoying little brother, Matt, went to Knoxville, Tennessee, native Jake Thomas. Jake's professional career had begun when he was just a baby—he made an appearance from his hospital bassinette during a local newscast just hours after he was born. His mother was a news anchor on the local evening news. Later on, Matt made slightly more memorable appearances in films like *A.I. Artificial Intelligence*, and *If Tomorrow Comes*.

While the kids in the show may have had limited professional experience, the actors chosen to play Lizzie's parents were longtime pros. Robert Carradine, the actor who plays Lizzie's dad, has been famous for more than twenty years. Before *Lizzie McGuire* he was best known for his starring role in *Revenge of the Nerds* and horror flicks like Stephen King's *Tommyknockers*. Hallie Todd, who plays Lizzie's mom, is also an accomplished actress, having appeared in TV movies like *Have You Ever Been Ashamed of Your Parents?* and *Who Will Love My Children?*, and several TV series including *Life with Roger*, *Going Places*, and *Murder, She Wrote*.

From day one Hilary felt at home on the *Lizzie McGuire* set. "We have a very kid- and pet-friendly set," she told *Girls' Life* magazine. "Our executive producer brings both his dogs, our medic brings his dog, Bear, and our wardrobe designer brings her dog, Pip. Are you sure they call this work?" she teased with a giggle.

Of course, Hilary was always aware that it was work. Her schedule made that tough to forget. During the filming of *Lizzie McGuire* she rarely had time to sit and hang out. She was in the majority of scenes in each episode. That meant memorizing a lot of lines, and spending a tremendous amount of time on the set. All of which led to a new "early to bed and early to rise" schedule for Hil.

"I get up at 5:30 A.M.," she explained to *Girls' Life*. "So I'm on the set by 7:00 A.M. Then it's wardrobe, hair, and makeup until 8:30. Then I either begin three hours of schoolwork with my tutor, or shoot our first scene. Thirty minutes for lunch, then animated Lizzie lines in the studio, back to shooting, and we end around 4:30. I have homework, lines to learn, and Tae Bo. I get to bed by 9:30."

Not exactly an easy life, is it?

Hilary agrees that her life is a lot less glamorous than it appears to people on the outside. In fact, in some ways it's a bit strange. "It's kind of weird," she told the Associated Press. "I go to work, then I go right up to school, and then I go and get changed, and then I keep going back and forth all day. But you get used to it."

Even with all the running back and forth from school to set, Hilary knew how lucky she was to be working on the *Lizzie McGuire* set. There was a certain magic to working on the old Desilu studio lot, where the most classic sitcom of all time, *I Love Lucy*, was once filmed.

And she loved her costars, especially Lalaine and Adam. The cast of the show quickly became sort of like her surrogate family. That was important to Hilary, because show business had been so disruptive to the lives of her real family members.

"The show does keep me away from my family," she explained to a chat audience. "I don't get to see my dad much, and my mom has to spend time away from my dad, and that's got to be hard."

Hilary's onscreen family has melded from time to time with her real family when Hil's big sis Haylie has guest starred on *Lizzie McGuire* as Kate's cousin Amy.

But Haylie's role as Amy is what's known as a recurring role. That means she is only on the show from time to time. Because of her long work hours, it seemed Hilary spent more time with her castmates than with her sister and her mother. Luckily, all the kids on the *Lizzie McGuire* set really got along well. Part of the reason Hil, Lalaine, and Adam were all so comfortable together was that Hil never pulled a star trip on her fellow actors or on the crew of the show. Sure, she was playing the title character, and was unquestionably the show's lead actress, but Hilary never saw it that way.

"Being an actor is a lot like playing sports at school," she told a chat audience. "You are part of a team and you have to behave that way."

Part of being on a team is being prepared. The kids of *Lizzie McGuire* learned early on that they had to know their lines and be ready to hit their marks when they came to work. (Not that there aren't foul-ups. Anyone who watches *Lizzie McGuire* regularly sees them as the credits roll at the end of the show.) Things had to run smoothly if the show was to stay on schedule. As Hilary explained it, "Because of time, we're all really prepared on the TV show. We usually do no more than three takes of any scene."

According to Hilary, memorizing lines is just like anything else: The more you do it, the easier it becomes. "It was hard when I started," she admitted to some fans during a Walt Disney Records chat. "But now I can pretty much look at the page and memorize the scene we're doing." Now that's a talent in itself.

Lizzie McGuire first hit the airwaves on January 19, 2001. It was instantly a success. Kids everywhere could relate to Lizzie's problems with her younger brother, Matt, her arguments with her evil nemesis, the popular Kate, and her crush on the junior-high hottie, Ethan. More importantly, kids saw themselves reflected in the character of Lizzie McGuire. And that made them love her.

Kids didn't just love Lizzie, though. They began to love Hilary herself. Suddenly it got harder and harder for Hil to go anywhere without being recognized. "I get a lot of attention from boys and girls who come up to me," she told *Girls' Life*. "They think they know me from the *Lizzie McGuire* show, and they all say, 'You're just like I thought.' I love meeting new people. When people come up to me and tell me they love my show, it makes me feel I'm doing something people like."

And it wasn't just kids who were approaching Hilary. As she told *E! Online*, "I don't think the Disney Channel gives us enough credit for the age range *Lizzie McGuire* actually has. College students come up to me, grandparents, famous people. It's really funny."

Hilary was genuinely surprised at how many people recognized her. She never thought of herself as a celebrity. "I think I'm a regular kid," she said at the time. "I never really think, 'Oh, I'm famous.' I'm still surprised when people recognize me."

Usually, Hilary likes meeting her fans. But there have been times where she's been overwhelmed by their appreciation.

"Haylie and I will tease her and say, 'Hey, Hil, we're going to get something to eat,'" Susan Duff told *Entertainment Weekly*. "'You want us to bring you something?'"

Hilary took the teasing in stride. She knew that meeting fans was part of the price you paid for fame. And Hil paid that price gladly. After all, fame has its benefits, too. For one thing, she got to use her fame to champion causes she believed in.

"The best part of being famous is it allows me to meet people and participate in events like I did this past spring with UNICEF and Kids with a Cause," she told a chat audience. "I got to meet Mr. Nelson Mandela and Mr. Kofi Annan."

She also got to work with some of Hollywood's most interesting and creative talents. In 2001, Hilary was cast as young Lila Jute in a small independent film called *Human Nature*.

Human Nature was a very off-beat film written by Charlie Kaufman, the screenwriter responsible for the quirky movie, *Being John Malkovich*. *Human*

Nature told the story of Nathan, a dead behavioral scientist, who narrates the movie from the Great Beyond. During his life, Nathan and his girlfriend Lila discovered a man who'd been raised completely in the wild. Nathan tried to help this man adapt to life in civilization, while Lila tried to allow him to keep his apelike past. It's a love triangle only mammals could get involved in.

Hilary was cast as a young Lila Jute as much for her talent as for her uncanny resemblance to the woman who played Lila as an adult—Patricia Arquette. Both actresses are big-eyed blondes with similar soft southern lilts to their voices.

Being cast in *Human Nature* was a big coup for Hilary. Although it was a film without a huge distribution, its cast included some of Hollywood's finest. Patricia Arquette had been in many independent and studio films including *Ed Wood*, *Little Nicky*, and *Lost Highway*. Tim Robbins, who played Nathan, was an Academy Award nominee, and had starred in such thought-provoking films as *The Shawshank Redemption*, *The Hudsucker Proxy*, and *Austin Powers, the Spy Who Shagged Me*. (Okay, so that one's not so thought-provoking, but it was awfully funny!)

Human Nature premiered on May 18, 2001, at the Cannes Film Festival. It went on to screen at film festivals around the world, eventually earning the

High Hopes Award at the Munich Film Festival, and The National Board of Review's Best Screenplay Award. Although it only grossed about $300,000 in the U.S., it was still a film Hilary could be proud of. Acting in *Human Nature* proved that Hil could play against type. She didn't always have to be perky Lizzie McGuire.

Still, it was Lizzie McGuire who was making Hilary Duff a household name. And for that she would be eternally grateful. So she was more than happy to return to the *Lizzie* set and begin work on more episodes.

| 5. | Out of Platforms and into a Uniform |

By the end of *Lizzie McGuire*'s first season, it had become abundantly clear that the Disney Channel had a hit on its hands. The Disney Company began working overtime taking advantage of the huge popularity of *Lizzie McGuire*. And let's face it, that's one company that knows how to market its best selling properties. Before long there were Lizzie McGuire dolls and *Lizzie McGuire* show soundtrack CDs on the shelves (Hilary recorded the song "Can't Wait" specially for the soundtrack, making it extra special for fans!). A huge clothing deal for Lizzie McGuire fashions was made with Limited Too, and a best-selling series of Lizzie McGuire books was launched.

But the company hadn't pulled all the rabbits out of its hat yet. There were big plans in store for the actress who played Lizzie as well. After all, not only was *Lizzie McGuire* a hit, but Hilary herself was a true star. The Disney folks decided to take advantage of her star power by sending Hilary and fellow Disney Channel superstar Christy Carlson Romano (Ren Stevens on *Even Stevens*) to military school in a made-for-TV movie called *Cadet Kelly*.

Cadet Kelly was a big departure for Hilary. Her character, Kelly Collins, starts out as a girl from New York's funky Greenwich Village, who's just "too cool for the rules!" She's hip to all the latest fashions and has a ton of friends. Her life is absolutely perfect— until her mother marries the head of the George Washington Military Academy in upstate New York. Suddenly this happy-go-lucky fashion plate finds herself in a military uniform without her lip gloss.

As if that weren't enough of a nightmare, Kelly soon learns that she's the target of an especially nasty upperclassman, Captain Jennifer Stone. Jennifer seems to really have it in for Kelly, and is determined to break her spirit. Jennifer was played by Hilary's real-life pal, Christy Carlson Romano.

Cadet Kelly was a really funny script written by veteran screenwriter Gail Parent, who, besides being a best-selling novelist, had penned scripts for classic sit-coms like *The Mary Tyler Moore Show* and *The Golden Girls*. It called for actresses who could pull off both humorous and serious scenes with equal talent, and who could learn to do real rifle drills like any other military school cadet. In the end, that would probably prove the hardest job for Hil and Christy to pull off.

The folks at the Disney Channel had no doubt that their two newest stars were up to the challenging, funny script. Gary Marsh, executive vice president of original programming at the Disney Channel told the press, "Hilary Duff and Christy Carlson Romano have established their comedy credentials in our two highest-rated original series. By showcasing them in a Disney Channel original movie, an even broader audience can now enjoy their comedic talents."

Hil and Christy both say they really enjoyed working with Gary Cole, the actor chosen to play Kelly's new stepdad. Gary has a long career in film. He's best known for his parts in *A Simple Plan*, *One Hour Photo*, *National Lampoon's American Adventure*, and *The Brady Bunch Movie*.

As soon as the movie was cast, Hilary was ready to go to work. She couldn't wait to get on the set of *Cadet Kelly*. But it would be a while before she was ready to start filming. There was a lot of pre-production work to be done on the film. And while that kind of work usually falls to the producers and designers, in this movie, Hilary and Christy would be doing plenty of pre-production work of their own.

Prior to filming *Cadet Kelly*, the girls enrolled in their very own boot camp, where they learned to behave like real military school cadets. "We had a week of intensive military training in the States, and then we went to Toronto for four more weeks of preparation before we started the movie," Hilary explained to a Disney chat audience. "It was great fun and I can arm wrestle with the best now."

But it wasn't all fun and games. There was plenty of hard work involved. While there's no doubt that Hilary and Christy didn't get the full boot camp treatment (let's face it—they're actresses, not recruits), they did have to learn some pretty intense drill team choreography, and the filming of the movie tested their athletic abilities to the max. "It was pretty challenging because I had to learn all the rifle drills and a lot of stunts," Hilary recalled. "But I loved it, and loved working with the producing team and the director." The fact that Hil was comfortable with director Larry Shaw came as no surprise. Larry had directed the first season of *Lizzie McGuire*.

Hilary was up to the challenge of *Cadet Kelly*. All those years of ballet performances gave her an edge when it came to the choreographed rifle drills, and her natural athletic ability came in handy with some of the scenes as well.

"I could cut it at boot camp," Hilary boasted to the chat audience. "As long as they don't take my lip gloss away. I'm pretty athletic, and I like a challenge. It was really a great experience to learn the rifle drills. I did all the drills myself and I really enjoyed the singular purpose of teamwork."

It took a lot of teamwork for Hilary and Christy to make *Cadet Kelly* not only fun, but believable. It was very important that the audience forget about their roles as Lizzie McGuire and Ren Stevens, and accept them as military school cadets with personalities that were quite different than their series' characters. That meant changing their expressions and making their performances believable in a military setting. It was no easy job (especially for Christy, whose *Even Stevens* character, Ren Stevens, is a nice girl, but whose character in *Cadet Kelly*, Jennifer Stone, was really mean). But their work was well worth the effort. When *Cadet Kelly* hit the Disney Channel airwaves in 2002, it became the highest rated original Disney Channel movie in the network's history!

Hilary discovered that in some ways she preferred working on a full-length movie to working on a TV show. As she told one chat audience, "I like the normalcy of a TV show, but I also like the challenge of a movie, creating a deeper character and a more detailed story."

It was no secret that Hilary hoped to do more film work, and it wasn't long before her wish was granted. Ironically, she found out about her next big film role while she was on the set of *Lizzie McGuire*.

6

Saving the World, and Other Secret Agent Tricks

Things were different when Hilary returned to the *Lizzie McGuire* set to shoot the new season. The cast knew they had a hit on their hands. Of course, that just made them want to work harder to keep the show as fun and entertaining as it always had been. The success of the show also brought in a whole slew of guest stars—famous fans of Lizzie McGuire who wanted to be part of the magic.

Famed rock and roll legend Steven Tyler, lead singer of Aerosmith, is a self-proclaimed huge fan of the show. He gave Hil and the gang an amazing Christmas present by actually donning a Santa Claus suit and singing for a Christmas episode. According to Hilary, that episode of *Lizzie McGuire* is her favorite of the sixty-five original episodes she worked on.

That doesn't come as a surprise to anyone who knows Hil. It's no secret Hilary loves Christmas. Her first album, which was released in 2002 was entitled, *Santa Claus Lane*. It was a collection of Christmas songs. "That was fun because it was my first experience in the recording studio," she told a Walt Disney Records chat audience. "And I got to do duets with Christina Milian and Lil' Romeo!"

Christmas may be Hil's fave time of year, but her experience on the *Lizzie McGuire* set brought her lots of exciting moments that had nothing to do with Santa. Hilary met her on-again, off-again boyfriend Aaron Carter when he stopped by to do an episode called "Aaron Carter Comes to Town." Hilary had to kiss Aaron on that episode, a moment which proved far more embarrassing than romantic. (How'd you like to kiss the world's cutest pop star in front of the entire crew of a TV show, knowing it was being filmed for the world to see?)

And it wasn't just musicians who were clamoring to join the *Lizzie* gang. Famous actors wanted in on the fun as well. They spanned all age groups. *Everybody Loves Raymond*'s Doris Roberts played Gordo's aunt Ruth in one episode, and Robert Carradine's half-brother, *Kung Fu* legend David Carradine, had a guest star role as well. Another time one of Hilary's close friends, Frankie Muniz, also popped by. Frankie, the star of Fox's *Malcolm in the Middle*, played himself in an episode that showed the tougher side of life as a star.

Hil and Frankie had a blast working together. Both kids were totally bummed when the episode was finished. They wished they could find a way to work together for a longer period of time.

Frankie was about to begin production on a new flick. There was a part in the film for a teenage girl who would be his love interest (or at the very least, the girl his character *wanted* to be his love interest). Frankie suggested Hilary for the part.

"Frankie was telling me about this cool teenage action spy movie he was going to do," Hil recalled on the official *Agent Cody Banks* Web site. "It sounded pretty exciting."

At the exact same time Frankie was telling Hilary about the movie, producer Dylan Sellers' eight-year-old daughter was recommending that her dad cast Hil in the film in the role of Natalie.

"You've just got to get Lizzie McGuire," Dylan recalled his daughter saying. "She's perfect!"

The next thing she knew, Hilary was meeting with Dylan and director Harald Zwart about playing the part of Natalie. Hilary liked the idea that although *Agent Cody Banks* was definitely Frankie's flick, the role of Natalie was central to the plot.

As Frankie Muniz described it in the movie's official Web site, "Cody Banks is just a normal kid to start with. He skateboards and goes to school. He went away to a camp where he was trained by the CIA when he was younger, and his parents and friends don't know anything about it. Then one day he gets called by the CIA and has this mission to do: to save the world. He's really excited, but his mission is to get to know this girl and have this girl like him."

That doesn't sound too hard does it? Unfortunately, while his CIA camp counselors may have trained Cody to drive wild cars, fly helicopters, and beat up people three times his size, they never taught him how to talk to girls. And that's what he needs if he's going to get close enough to Natalie to uncover her father's diabolical scheme to create an army of indestructible robots.

As the movie opens, Cody's not exactly suave and sophisticated—he's more of a dork. That doesn't impress the popular Natalie one bit. Hilary recalled on the movie's Web site, "Natalie is a normal fourteen-year-old. When she first meets Cody, he gets shy and starts stuttering and asking really dumb questions. She doesn't want to have anything to do with him."

Of course, as happens in all great movies, that changes, and Natalie is eventually taken with Cody.

Hilary loved the film, and she had a blast making it. But she wasn't one hundred percent satisfied with her part. "I was really envious of Frankie Muniz when we were shooting *Agent Cody Banks*," she told one magazine. "He was getting to do all the stunts and all the martial arts fighting . . . I was the just playing the girlfriend, so I basically just had to stand around."

Still, Hilary managed to steal every scene she was in—even without the help of fancy gadgets or expensive cars. She only had her natural charisma to work with. In Hilary's case, that was more than enough!

Harald Zwart was really impressed with the two young actors he directed in the film. "Cody has a quadruple life," he explained. "He pretends to Natalie that he's a normal kid. He pretends to the CIA that he's in control of everything. Then he actually starts to fall in love with this girl, and at home he's trying to conceal the fact that he's a secret agent. There are quite a few levels to Frankie's performance and he's great at juggling all those things."

Harald was equally impressed with Hilary's take on Natalie. "Hilary's a star," he said on the *Agent Cody Banks* Web site. "When she's on the screen, she's radiant. It's easy to understand why Cody goes through everything just to rescue her. She has a great sense of humor and great warmth and beauty."

When *Agent Cody Banks* was released on March 16, 2003, it was greeted with mixed reviews.

Although critics universally applauded the performances of Frankie and Hilary, they felt the film's spy-kid theme was too close to the movie *Spy Kids*. Luckily, few of Hil and Frankie's fans bother to read newspaper reviews. In the end, *Agent Cody Banks*, a movie which cost about $26 million to make, earned nearly double that in its initial U.S. release. Add video receipts and overseas markets to that, and you have a minor hit on your hands!

Hilary wasn't surprised that kids liked the movie. After all, she's a kid, and she loved it. Especially the special effects. She told *TeenHollywood.com* that "the best part of the movie was at the end when everything was getting blown up. It was cool to see behind the scenes how they actually did it."

Agent Cody Banks reinforced Hilary's star status in Hollywood, because it showed that she could help bring in audiences. Sure, it was really Frankie's big film, but plenty of fans were flocking to the theaters to see Hil.

Hilary was unaware of all her newfound success. By the time *Agent Cody Banks* went into release, Hilary had already finished her next film (*The Lizzie McGuire Movie*) and was busy working on yet another (*Cheaper By the Dozen*). She didn't have time to realize that she had now become a movie star.

As she told a reporter for ABC news, "I haven't

had much time off lately, and I went to the movies with my friend and I saw a *Cody Banks* poster . . . and I was like 'Oh my God!' You just forget about it, you know, and then you're like 'Wow, that's cool!'"

Audiences couldn't forget about Hilary's star power. Kids everywhere looked up to her, a fact which never failed to shock her. "It's weird to think people look up to me," she told one fan magazine. "And when kids started saying they were dressing as me for Halloween, that was so weird."

But it wasn't weird to Hil's fans. They adored her. And they made it clear that they wanted to see her on the big screen more often. They were in luck. Two months later Hilary's next big film hit the screens nationwide. The character she played in this one was far more familiar to her (and her fans) than Natalie was.

The character's name was Lizzie McGuire.

7

Lizzie Goes *Rome*-in'

By mid 2002, all sixty-five original first run episodes of *Lizzie McGuire* were completed. There were definite changes in the later episodes. Lizzie and her friends had grown up, just as Hilary, Adam, and Lalaine had in real life.

"We all look so much younger in the first shows," Hilary recalled to *Girls' Life* magazine in the spring of 2002. "But Lizzie and her friends are growing up just like anyone else, and the new season will be amped up a bit from last year."

Indeed, the producers were preparing Lizzie and her pals for a big step in their lives. The last season of the show corresponded with Lizzie's last year in middle school. By the final episode, Lizzie, Miranda, Gordo, Kate, Ethan, and Larry had gone through everything soon-to-be middle school grads could—dances, arguments, and the fear of moving on. The only thing they hadn't experienced was graduation. The show's producers were saving that big event for something special—*The Lizzie McGuire Movie*! (Okay, so it's not the most original title ever, but it gets the message across.)

The Lizzie McGuire Movie was designed to begin with Lizzie's graduation from middle school. She shares the experience with *almost* all of her school friends. Lalaine wasn't available to be in the movie, so her character, Miranda, is supposed to be visiting relatives out of the country.

Although the movie was aimed at fans of the TV show, according to Hilary you don't have to be a *Lizzie McGuire* addict to understand what was going on in the film.

"It does pick up where the show left off," she explained to ABC news, "but you don't have to have watched the TV show to know what the movie is about or to know what *Lizzie McGuire* is about. It kind of gives you the picture right off the bat."

Does it ever! Just in case you didn't know Matt was a real pain in the neck, the movie starts with him secretly taping Lizzie, just so he can embarrass her. And if you'd been living under a rock and didn't know that Lizzie could be the world's biggest klutz, once you saw her single-handedly destroy her class's graduation by tripping over her own feet, you got the message loud and clear. When it comes to Lizzie McGuire, some things never change.

And that's how it should be. As Stan Rogow, one of the producers of the *Lizzie McGuire Movie* explained to ABC news, "Lizzie's emotional struggles are universal. "What we've done with the movie is to make the adventure bigger for the big screen, and deepened those emotions."

But as much as things may stay the same for Lizzie, things have to change as well. Let's face it, the emotions and experiences middle schoolers have are different than those which high schoolers must face. And in *The Lizzie McGuire Movie*, high school is the next stop. That meant that Lizzie was going to have become more independent and even add a little romance to her life.

The Lizzie McGuire Movie was just the vehicle to show Lizzie growing up. From its earliest planning stages, the movie was going to be about Lizzie gaining some independence and heading off for a school trip during summer vacation.

The question was, where should the producers send Lizzie? They tossed around several places, including Hawaii. But in the end, they decided on Rome. There could be no better city for Lizzie's first stab at love.

(Here's a little known factoid: Once the directors had chosen Rome for the film's location, they temporarily decided to call the movie *Ciao, Lizzie*. Eventually they went back to *The Lizzie McGuire Movie*.)

Speaking of love, if Lizzie was going to fall for someone (other than Ethan, that is) he was going to have to be someone special. Someone cute and talented, and since the movie took place in Rome, someone from . . . *Florida*. Yes, that's right, Lizzie's Italian love interest was played by American Yani Gellman. Not that you'd ever know Yani was from the States. His accent in the movie was impeccable. He worked with a voice coach to make sure that he sounded like a real Italian.

Yani had been a student of different accents and cultures for most of his life. "When I was younger I moved around a lot," he said on the Web site for *Guinevere Jones*, a short-lived TV series he starred in. "I was born in Florida, moved to Australia, where I lived in Sydney for five years, then onto Spain, after that, Toronto, next Texas, then back to Toronto."

All that moving around may have been hard on Yani as a child, but it came in handy when he joined the cast of *The Lizzie McGuire Movie* on the set. Those kids had already worked together for two years. They were close friends. Once again Yani was the new kid. But his experience with moving around had taught him how to make friends quickly.

Hilary in particular spent a lot of time making the newcomer feel welcome. It was important that Yani and she get along well. After all, their onscreen romance had to be believable. And while there was no romance off the set, the two did become good friends, which helped spark that fiery chemistry audiences witnessed on the screen.

Yani's adjustment to the *The Lizzie McGuire Movie* set was also helped along because over the years he'd had roles in several Disney Channel productions, including the TV movie *Tru Confessions*, and a guest appearance on the TV series *The Famous Jett Jackson*. So he was very familiar with the type of kid-friendly, happy set *The Lizzie McGuire Movie* utilized.

Yani wasn't the only one during the shoot who had to spend time with a vocal coach learning to mimic a perfect Italian accent. Hilary had to do the same thing. That's because she played two roles in *The Lizzie McGuire Movie*—Lizzie, and her Italian hottie's singing partner, Isabella.

Confused? Well, it all makes sense when you consider the story of *The Lizzie McGuire Movie*. In the film, Lizzie, Gordo, Ethan, and Kate all wind up on the same post-graduation trip to Rome. It's supposed to be an educational experience, but Lizzie's education begins to lean more toward romance when she discovers that she bears an unbelievable resemblance to an Italian singer named Isabella.

Isabella is famous in Italy for her recordings and performances with her performing partner, Paolo. But Isabella has suddenly disappeared and Paolo is afraid he'll have to cancel an upcoming concert. Then he spots Lizzie and thinks his problems are solved. All he has to do is train Lizzie to pretend to be Isabella and perform at the concert.

But there's something odd about Paolo and his sudden attraction to Lizzie McGuire. Of course Lizzie can't see that. Neither can Kate, who finds Lizzie's Italian romance exciting—if completely unfair. (Shouldn't *she* be the one riding around Rome on a Vespa? After all, she's the popular one!) Only Gordo can see that this Paolo has something up his sleeve. The question is, what? (Forget it. You won't find the answer to that one here—you'll have to rent the movie to find out!)

Playing Lizzie wasn't tough for Hil—she's used to being in her klutzy alter ego's skin. But taking on the personality of Isabella was something altogether different.

"Isabella is this very confident singer with big, wild, crazy dark hair. So it was a big change for me. And she had the accent, so it was a little hard for me to do," she explained.

Working on *The Lizzie McGuire Movie* wasn't all that different from working on the show. Sure, the cast was in Rome, and a lot of the movie was shot against the magnificent Italian backdrop. But everyone was just as professional as they were when they were working back home, and for the most part, each scene in the movie was completed in three to five takes. That's pretty unusual for a major motion picture, in which scenes can be shot and reshot over and over and over again. But this cast was used to a TV schedule, and they were able to adjust to a much faster pace.

What Hilary wasn't used to was performing in front of a huge crowd. But at the climax of *The Lizzie McGuire Movie*, that's exactly what she had to do. Hil admitted that got her very nervous. "I've never done much performing, so like, I don't know, it's weird," she told ABC news. "It was fun though, really, really great dancers and cool outfits, and the song had so much energy in it!"

While the other kids network, Nickelodeon, had been turning their TV shows into big-screen productions for a long time, *The Lizzie McGuire Movie* was the first Disney Channel show to become a feature film. And the studio went all out to promote the movie. In the weeks before the film's May 2 release, Hilary found herself flying all over the country promoting the film, and her single from the soundtrack, which was entitled, "Why Not?" She jetted to New York, where she appeared on *Good Morning America*, *Live with Regis and Kelly*, *The Early Show*, and MTV's *TRL*, where Hil appeared as a guest host. More than four thousand fans blocked the streets of Times Square just to get a glimpse of Hil doing her hosting duties. The next day she did an autograph signing at the huge Disney Store on New York's Fifth Avenue, and sat for interviews and photo shoots for magazines like *Vanity Fair* and *Entertainment Weekly*.

Hilary may have seemed calm and cool during her interviews, but the truth was she was anything but. She had good reason to be stressed. After all, while Hil had been in movies before, she'd never been the star (other than in *Casper Meets Wendy*— and even there she shared the billing with a ghost!). This was the first time the success of a movie depended on her.

"It's hard, because *Agent Cody Banks* was really Frankie's movie," she told CBS's *The Early Show*. "So he could be nervous for that one. But now I'm getting pretty nervous."

But the folks at Disney weren't at all stressed. They'd seen how the audience reacted at a preview screening of *The Lizzie McGuire Movie*. "When we previewed *The Lizzie McGuire Movie*, the title went up and people started to cheer and you'd think we were sitting in *Star Wars*," Nina Jacobson, Disney's president of production, told *USA Today*.

Posters for the movie went up everywhere—from city billboards to the backs of buses. Ads for the movie played on the Disney Channel and its sister networks ABC and ABC Family Channel. Trailers began to appear in movie theaters. You couldn't go anywhere without seeing Hilary's shining face smiling at you, announcing *The Lizzie McGuire Movie*. The Hollywood premiere, just a few days before the film officially opened, brought out the fans and the press. Hilary's date for the premiere, Aaron Carter, sparked new rumors that their romance was on again. But Hilary was discreet. She just told the press, "You'll have to ask him."

The question no one was asking was, will fans come out for the film? As far as Disney was concerned, the answer was a definite yes. And they were right. The movie opened on May 2, 2003, and would end up earning 17 million dollars in its first weekend alone. That was pretty incredible, considering its main competition was *X2: X-Men United*, one of the summer season's earliest blockbusters. The film continued to stay in the top five for several weeks, even though other blockbusters like *Matrix Reloaded* were released as well.

Reviews for *The Lizzie McGuire Movie* were

mixed, although Hilary's personal reviews were great. It didn't matter whether critics liked the film overall; everyone was unanimous in their praise for her. As the *Atlanta Journal-Constitution* said, "Adolescent girls will love watching Hilary do her thing." The *Cincinnati Enquirer* echoed that sentiment, saying, "*The Lizzie McGuire Movie* exists . . . to showcase its lovely young star and that it does very well indeed." The *L.A. Times* review was also typical of the critics' reaction nationwide, saying that "Duff's baby bombshell exuberance is the . . . reason you keep watching *The Lizzie McGuire Movie*."

Kids did keep watching the film—over and over again. And each time they saw it, girls swooned over Lizzie's romance with Paolo, and boys laughed at her clumsiness and the hijinks of the tour group's wacky school principal. It truly was a film with something for everyone.

The success of the *The Lizzie McGuire Movie* also gave Hilary's recording career a big push. Hil has always loved singing and was already in the process of recording her second album, *Metamorphosis*, when *The Lizzie McGuire Movie* hit theaters. Her single from *The Lizzie McGuire Movie* soundtrack, "Why Not?" started to get regular airplay on Radio Disney and other Top 40 stations. It eventually reached number six on MTV's *TRL*, thanks to the millions of phone calls from Hil's fans, requesting that the song remain on the show's top ten. That was no small accomplishment, since "Why Not?" shared the top ten with hits by established singing sensations like Christina Aguilera, Justin Timberlake, and Avril Lavigne.

Hilary's relationship with MTV continued long after her guest hosting duties on *TRL* were over. Thanks in part to her video's success on MTV, and the success of *The Lizzie McGuire Movie*, Hilary was asked to be a presenter on MTV's Movie Awards on Saturday, May 31, 2003.

Being asked to be a presenter on the MTV Movie Awards was proof of just how much Hilary had grown up. The audience for MTV was a far cry from the kids who loved her as Lizzie McGuire. Being a presenter on the show meant that Hil now had the star power to attract kids, tweens, teens, and even the twenty-something crowd that watched MTV religiously.

As all the excitement swirled around her, Hilary seemed unfazed. That was partly because her family would never allow her to get a swelled head. It was also because Hilary was too busy working on her next project to even notice that she was rapidly becoming the hottest thing in Hollywood. At that moment, she was just part of a big crowd of kids— twelve kids to be exact. All of whom had parts in the movie *Cheaper by the Dozen*.

8. | *Dozen* This Seem Fun?

Cheaper by the Dozen's director, Shawn Levy, had spent a lot of time working on TV shows and made-for-TV movies that aired on the Disney Channel. Most notably, he had directed *The Famous Jett Jackson* TV series, and the made-for-TV movie, *Jett Jackson: The Movie*. He'd also directed episodes of the network's show *So Weird*.

So it was no shock that Shawn was hoping to get Hilary Duff to take part in his latest film venture, a big screen flick called *Cheaper by the Dozen*. He was well aware of the success she had single-handedly brought to the cable network, and was anxious to have her be part of his film. In order to woo Hil to his set, Shawn had a part created just for her.

Cheaper by the Dozen was based on an old book

about the Gilbreth family who lived in New Jersey in the 1910s and 1920s. The book, written by two of the twelve Gilbreth children, told the story of their family, and focused especially on how their dad, Frank, ran the house. The real-life Frank Gilbreth was a pioneer in the field of motion study and efficiency. One of his jobs was to analyze how factory workers could perform their jobs more efficiently. He sometimes applied his theories to his house, often with hilarious results.

The book *Cheaper by the Dozen* was a huge hit when it was first published. In 1950 it was turned into a film for the first time, starring classic movie actors Myrna Loy and Clifton Webb as the parents. That movie stayed very close to the plot of the book.

The folks at Twentieth Century Fox first began talking about making a new *Cheaper by the Dozen* in 1998. It took nearly four years to get a script that the studio, and star Steve Martin, were happy with. The new script was no longer about Frank Gilbreth, efficiency expert. It was about Tom Baker, small town football coach, and his wife Mary, played by film and TV comedienne Bonnie Hunt. In the new movie Tom is offered a chance to coach a Big Ten football team at the exact time that his wife publishes her first book and goes out on a publicity tour, leaving Tom to deal with work and their twelve children. All these changes in Tom and Mary's careers force them to change their parenting styles, too—and they discover that their ideas on child-rearing aren't always compatible.

Besides Steve Martin and Bonnie Hunt, the cast includes Tom Welling, better known as the young Clark Kent/Superman on TVs *Smallville*. Tom was cast as the eldest Baker child. Film actress Piper Perabo, best known for her work in the movie *Coyote Ugly*, was cast as Anne Baker, the oldest girl. Piper's on-screen love interest was to be portrayed by none other than super-hot TV and movie star Ashton Kutcher.

It was a pretty impressive line up, which explains why Hilary was thrilled when Shawn Levy had the part of middle daughter Lorraine Baker created just for her. Hil quickly signed on to the project, and was there on the set when filming began in March, 2003. She was thrilled to be sharing a set with such huge talent. As she told TV's *Extra*, "I'm so excited! This is the best thing that's ever happened to me!"

Hilary had a blast working on *Cheaper by the Dozen*. Just like at *Lizzie McGuire*, there were lots of kids on the set. Shawn Levy made sure that this set was also kid friendly. He had a lot of experience working with kids (besides *The Famous Jett Jackson* work he'd done, Shawn had worked on kid-populated shows like *Lassie* and *Animorphs*), and he knew how to keep child actors happy while they were working.

For Hilary's part, she learned to while away the long breaks between takes by playing her new fave computer game—*The Simms*. As she told fans on her Web site, she not only became "totally hooked" on the game during shooting, she managed to turn most of the rest of the cast onto it as well.

Although she loved working in Rome during the filming of *The Lizzie McGuire Movie*, Hilary was happy to be able to be on a set that was closer to home. *Cheaper by the Dozen* was filmed entirely in California (although she did have to leave her Southern California home for a few days of shooting in the northern part of the state), and was totally convenient for her. Not only was Hil able to commute from her own house instead of a hotel, she was able to continue recording her new album, *Metamorphosis*, while she worked on the movie.

"At least everything is happening in town," she told fans who logged onto her official Web site. "I don't have to travel right now."

Filming on *Cheaper by the Dozen* concluded in June 2003, just in time for Hilary to begin preliminary promotion for *Metamorphosis*. Although the album wasn't due to hit stores until fall, she was anxious to whet her fans' appetite for new Hilary Duff music. Hilary began a publicity blitz for the album in June, 2003, making stops in New York City, Tampa, Fort Lauderdale, Miami, and Denver. She debuted two cuts, "Party Up" and "Voice in My Head," on New York City's top-forty radio station Z-100, and her fans called up to add their voices to her interview—naturally, they loved what they heard.

At the same time, Hilary was getting ready to start her next film, *The Cinderella Story*, in which she had the title role. The film was in pre-production, but that still meant that Hil had to go to meetings, costume fittings, and all the other events that lead up to the actual filming of movie.

Oh yeah, and to top it all off, she had to do her schoolwork, answer questions from fans on her Web site, and study for her driving exam.

And you thought the life of a superstar was easy!

9. | A Week in the Life

In fact, the life of a superstar can get very complicated. "Sometimes I won't even know what I'm doing the next day, and I'll have to go do it and be told right before I run on," Hilary admitted to *Entertainment Weekly*. "But you know, I really don't like to not work."

It's a good thing Hilary's so into her work. Lately she hasn't had time to do much of anything else. Here's a look at her schedule for a week in late April and early May 2003, the days surrounding the release of both *The Lizzie McGuire Movie* and her single, "Why Not?"

WARNING: Just reading this chapter can cause exhaustion!

***

April 29:

Hilary was busy working on the *Cheaper by the Dozen* set in California, but her mind was in New York. "Why Not?" had already premiered on MTV's *TRL*, and she was getting ready to fly to New York to promote both the movie and the music.

April 30:

Hilary shot a few more scenes for *Cheaper by the Dozen*, then boarded a plane bound for New York City. Her mom and Haylie came along for the adventure. Hil hoped her plane would get in before midnight, so she could get in a little shut eye before beginning her whirlwind promotional tour of the city.

As she flew, Hilary did homework and answered letters sent to her Web site from fans.

May 1:

Hilary arrived in New York shortly after midnight, but she seemed wide awake and excited when she hosted *TRL* that afternoon. As Hilary recalled it in her online diary, "I'm excited and nervous at the same time." The excitement was evident, but Hilary managed to keep her nerves in check.

May 2:

It was Friday morning, and Hilary was up with the sun so she could get to ABC studios in time for an appearance on *Good Morning America*, followed by a chat with Regis Philbin and Kelly Ripa on *Live with Regis and Kelly*.

May 3:

Her fans had been lining up since before sunrise, so Hilary knew she couldn't complain about being tired as she arrived at the massive Disney Store on New York's famed Fifth Avenue on Saturday morning. In fact, she stayed forty-five minutes later than she should have to meet as many people as she possibly could before finally leaving for a photo shoot which began at two o'clock. After hours of makeup, hair, and flashbulbs erupting in her face, Hilary headed back to the hotel to pack. She had an early morning flight back to L.A. the next day.

May 4:

Other kids might be relaxing on a Sunday, but not Hil. She had to study lines for her next day of shooting on the *Cheaper by the Dozen* set and do her homework during the flight back to L.A.

May 6:

On Monday morning, Hilary was back on the set, hanging with the eleven other kids who play her sibs in *Cheaper by the Dozen*. She was also tutored for three hours and did some phone interviews with magazines. When she got home from the set, she worked on homework and prepped for a radio appearance on Los Angeles's KIIS FM. She was slated to take over the station's playlist for an hour, and play her personal faves, including "Why Not?" (natch!).

Hilary finished shooting her role in *Cheaper by the Dozen* on May 10, 2003. But she didn't have time to relax. She went right back into the studio to continue her work on *Metamorphosis*. She'd already recorded five songs, and the plan was for her to have eight more finished by the end of May. Somewhere in there, she was going to have to find time for rehearsals for the MTV Movie Awards, since she was going to be a presenter at the network's May 31 awards show.

But hey, Hil's got it all under control. For her, it's just another day's (or make that another month's) work.

| 10. | Peer into the Crystal Ball |

Hilary has already starred in a hit TV show, headlined in several major motion pictures, and recorded two solo albums. So, where does a girl go from here?

It doesn't seem as though Hilary's momentum will be ending anytime soon. As soon as shooting on *Cheaper by the Dozen* wrapped, Hilary was back on a movie set, this time starring in *The Cinderella Story*, a romantic fantasy slated to hit theaters in 2004. *The Cinderella Story* was a bit of departure for Hilary. Gone were all the makeup and funky clothes. She had to depend on her acting talent to keep the audience intrigued.

"It's a really great story because it's a new-age Cinderella story," Hil told *TeenHollywood.com*. "It's a totally different character than I've ever played before. Lizzie McGuire was really into makeup and hair and clothes and whatever the style was. Same with Natalie in *Cody Banks*. She was a very popular girl at school and she had everything going for her. I think *The Cinderella Story* is different. She's very independent. She's a plain Jane and she has a metamorphosis. I'm hoping it will appeal to a little bit older audience."

Even more exciting is that Hilary's mother will be executive producing this film. Hilary told *Teenmag.com* that she's glad her mom will be making some of the big decisions. "She gets to say 'I kind of think it's this way or that way.' She can have more input."

She had other films in the works as well, including one reportedly penned by Freddie Prinze Jr., with a part the super hottie had written just for her. Can you imagine the screams Hilary let loose when she heard about that?!

As for music, Hilary isn't about to let the pop momentum stop. She had a huge hit with "Why Not?", which reached as high as number six on *TRL*. She's hoping to build on that success when her second solo album, *Metamorphosis*, is released. To help boost sales, she's planning to crisscross the country once again, to promote the album. Fans might be shocked at the sound of the CD, however. Hilary's publicist has described it as having "slightly more mature songs," than Hilary has recorded in the past. (But don't expect anything like Christina Aguilera and Britney Spears' sudden change from teen queens to sexy women; Hilary's still Hilary after all. She's just growing up a bit.)

Changing her sound might seem risky, but Hilary knows what she's doing. Hilary's fans are getting older, and their tastes are changing. Hilary's in a great position to know what teens like to listen to—after all, she's a teen herself.

Hilary's comfortable with a lot of the music because several songs have been written by her big sis, Haylie. "She's an amazing writer," Hilary told *TeenHollywood.com*. "I don't think I could sit down and write a whole song because it's so hard to get the form down and write the chorus and the pre chorus, and the verse and the bridge." Which is not to say that Hilary was left out of the song-writing process altogether. She collaborated with several writers on *Metamorphosis*.

According to Hilary, the album's general sound is best described as "kind of a mix between pop and rock, edging more to the rock side," which is exactly where she told *TeenHollywood.com* that her own preference leans. The first single from the album, "So Yesterday," was released in July, 2003. Hilary shot the video for the single on Venice Beach in downtown L.A.

Hilary doesn't see any reason why she shouldn't be able to combine acting and singing in her multi-faceted life. Like one of her idols, Jennifer Lopez, Hilary has a need to create in many venues.

And speaking of J Lo, Hilary has followed in the diva's footsteps at the mall as well. J Lo was one of the first singer-actresses to create a line of clothing aimed directly at her fans. Hilary's coming out with her own clothing called Stuff by Hilary Duff, which will include everything from shoes to blow dryers. She's also in the planning stages of introducing a makeup line created by Townley cosmetics that will include Hilary Duff lip gloss and eye makeup.

Movies, records, makeup, shoes . . . Hilary's one busy teen queen. So does all this mean the demise of Lizzie McGuire? Unfortunately, that's what it looks like. When *The Lizzie McGuire Movie* hit theaters in May 2003, it was believed that the TV show had run its course. But when the movie became a huge hit, the Disney folks suddenly seemed reluctant to let go of Lizzie. Rumors swirled that the company was trying to convince Hilary to come back for more adventures—this time in high school. According to the Hollywood buzz, the Walt Disney Company not only wanted Hilary to star in more episodes of the TV show (which could possibly air during prime time on the Disney-owned ABC network rather than the Disney Channel, hopefully giving a ratings boost to the struggling network), they were prepared to go right to work creating a sequel to the film. In fact, the day *The Lizzie McGuire Movie* opened, the *Hollywood Reporter* featured an article that said Disney had hired *Lizzie McGuire* writer Melissa Gould to write the sequel. That was an unusual bit of news considering the original *Lizzie McGuire Movie* had been penned by the series' executive producer Susan Estelle Jansen along with Ed Decter and John Strauss. Melissa had been a writer on the TV series. The reason for the change in writing staff was a mystery, especially since the Disney folks wouldn't make any kind of statement about a sequel.

In fact nothing about Lizzie McGuire's future was certain, other than the fact that getting Hilary back was going to cost the Disney folks—big time! Originally, Hilary was believed to earn about fifteen thousand dollars an episode for the TV show. (At least according to the *Wall Street Journal*—Hilary's reps don't talk publicly about her salary.) In order for Hilary to return to the *Lizzie McGuire* set, her representatives (including her mom) were rumored to be asking about $100,000 per episode. As for a sequel to *The Lizzie McGuire Movie*, the *Wall Street Journal* reported that Hilary's reps were asking for a five-million-dollar paycheck. That was five times what Hilary had earned to play Lizzie in the first movie.

Unfortunately, despite days and weeks of intense contract negotiations, Hilary and Disney never could agree to a deal. According to a report on *E! Online*, the Walt Disney Company severed ties with Hil just before Memorial Day Weekend 2003, unable to meet the pay raise demands. (Hilary says the decision wasn't all about money. According to her Web site, it had more to do with "the working environment.") From now on, Lizzie McGuire's fans would have to see her in reruns of the original sixty-five episodes, or on the video and DVD release of *The Lizzie McGuire Movie*.

Even though she's bid adieu to Lizzie McGuire, Hilary's fans will never have to go anywhere without her again. In May 2003, Hasbro Toys announced that Hilary had signed on to be the spokesperson for their new VideoNow personal video player, which kids could carry with them on their belts or in their backpacks. (Think HitClips with pictures.) She made a short film called "A Day in the Life of Hilary Duff" especially for VideoNow, and was planning additional videos as well. Hilary loved the product. "I can't wait to get one myself," she said in a Hasbro press release.

Although Hil's comedic timing and talent has been universally praised by both fans and the press, in the summer of 2003 she expressed an interest to take her career in a more serious direction. "There are tons and tons of projects that I really want to do," Hilary told the *New York Daily News*. "The drama stuff—I want everyone to know I can do that."

Not that that means Hil is planning on abandoning her fans. As she explained to *USA Today*, drama doesn't have to mean an R rating.

"I want to show people I can do more than just be Lizzie McGuire," she said. "But that doesn't mean you have to be edgy. I don't have to play a pregnant mother on crack. You can play a dramatic role without being too edgy."

As long as Susan Duff is in charge of her daughter's career, Hil won't have to worry about her roles being too edgy. According to Rich Ross, president of entertainment and Disney Channel, "Hilary is working very hard with her mom to pick appropriate roles. If the parents stay involved and the kids are comfortable with acting, then they choose vehicles that are appropriate."

But that doesn't mean that Hilary is going to keep taking happy comedic roles. Her mother is willing to let her stretch her dramatic wings—in the right part, of course. Which means we could be seeing Hilary in a dramatic or action role in the near future. And for all we know, Hilary, the ultimate *Charlie's Angels* fan, would love to have a little butt kicking in her movie future.

There's already a Lizzie McGuire doll. Could there be a Hilary Duff action figure in the future? Well, as the song says, why not?

11. | A Lovable Libra!

Hilary's September 28 birthday means that her sun sign is Libra (September 22–October 23). Sun sign is definitely the right word for Hilary and other Libras. People born under this sign are positive thinkers who tend to look on the bright side of life. They love nature, and strive to surround themselves with beautiful things. (Which may explain Hilary's love of clothing, shoes, and accessories. She feels good about herself when she's wearing beautiful things.).

Libras are known for their gift of gab. They can make conversation with anyone, and frequently will. For someone in the public eye like Hilary, that characteristic can come in pretty handy. Hil's always meeting new people. In typical Libra fashion, she often finds their lives more interesting than her own.

She loves meeting and greeting fans at autograph sessions or during online chats, and often asks them a ton of questions about their lives, as well as clue-ing them in on what's new in hers.

Libras are team players. They love being part of a group. That's what made shooting *Cheaper by the Dozen* so much fun for Hil. As she told *Entertainment Tonight*, "There's always someone here to talk to or hang out with. It's so much fun."

Hilary had a similar experience on the *Lizzie McGuire* set. Although many teen actors say that being on a set is difficult because they lose big chunks of their childhood, Hilary's never had that problem. For starters, there were lots of teens on the *Lizzie* set. They hung out together, studied together, and yes, shopped together. In many ways, the *Lizzie McGuire* set was Hilary's middle school—without all the pettiness and cliques that can take place in regu-lar middle schools. That's a good thing, because Libras are not prone to cliquish behavior. They tend to be very inclusive sorts who want to be friends with everyone they meet.

Hilary's well aware that she's lucky to have avoided some of the popularity problems her TV alter-ego Lizzie McGuire has been faced with. "I haven't gone to junior high because I was tutored on the set," she told a chat audience, "but I wouldn't have been most popular because I've never liked cliques."

Libra is the sign of the scales, and most Libras are very balanced people. They are able to keep things in perspective, and maintain order in their lives. That's an important characteristic for a girl like Hilary, who's so busy. In typical Libra fashion, she's able to balance her home life with her work life. Her school-work gets done (even if it has to sometimes be sent to her tutor by e-mail), she makes sure she's got time to swim, shop, and hang with her pals, and she's always prepared on the set. It takes a special kind of person to juggle a schedule like that and manage to successfully keep all those balls in the air.

Of all the signs in the zodiac, Libras are the most objective. They're able to see the whole picture, and make their decisions based on a variety of facts. But objective doesn't mean decisive. Libras tend to fluctuate back and forth for ages until they make a decision. Luckily Hilary has her parents to help her decide which scripts to choose and which products to endorse. Hilary knows that having her folks in her corner is a great thing. They only want the best for her, and will never steer her wrong. *New York Post* columnist Cindy Adams recently called Susan Duff the "gold standard in stage moms," because she's Hilary's greatest advocate.

Libras are not driven by ego or conceit. They're driven by a true of love of what they do. Hilary has always loved performing, whether it be acting, singing, or dancing. That's what makes her get up in the morning with a smile on her face. For Hilary, it's not about the fame and fortune. (She recently told one chat audience that she hasn't got a "mansion or limousine. I'm not into things like that.") Rather, Hilary just likes having fun on the set. "I'm pretty young, so I don't think of it as work," she told *E! Online*. "It's just fun to be part of the whole process."

Libras are known perfectionists, and they are devoted to what they do. They're determined to get things done with excellence. Hilary never comes to work unprepared. She's got her lines down before she ever hits the set. Perfectionism has its downside, though. After all, no one's perfect. Hilary seems to be coming to grips with that reality. She's learned to laugh at her own mistakes, as anyone who watches the bloopers at the end of each *Lizzie McGuire* can tell you.

When it comes to romance, Libras love to be loved. They're happiest when they're involved in a romance. A Libra without a love interest is like a fish out of water. That's why Libras are always searching for the perfect mate. But being a Libra's dream date isn't easy. A Libra lover has to be romantic and unafraid to be affectionate both in public and in private. Libras are big huggers and snugglers. Romantic walks along the beach are a Libra's idea of heaven, since they appeal to their love of romance and nature. Anyone who's involved with a Libra like Hilary had better be prepared to pay her a few compliments. Libras love that—as long as the compliments are sincere. They can see right through phoniness. Libras also value honesty and loyalty. They're not into being involved with players (which explains Hilary's reluctance to get too involved with Aaron Carter.)

The guy who finally snags Hil's heart will be one lucky dude. Like all easygoing Libras, Hilary's known for being wonderful to be around. All she needs to be happy is a guy who will understand and appreciate the real Hilary Duff. And when she finds a guy like that, this lucky Libra is sure to live in harmony and peace.

We'll bet you think Hilary Ann Duff is number one. A perfect 10 in both looks and talent.

Well, won't you be surprised when you find out that Hil's actually a four! That's right, a perfect *four*—at least in numerology. The letters in Hilary Ann Duff's name make her a four in this ancient science.

Numerology started with the ancient Babylonians. According to numerology, each person's personality falls into one of nine categories. You can find out what category your favorite star (which would be Hilary—of course!) fits into by counting up the numbers that correspond with the letters in her name.

How did we figure out Hil was a four? We wrote out all of the letters in Hilary's full name (nicknames don't work in numerology), and then matched the letters to this chart.

1	2	3	4	5	6	7	8	9
A	B	C	D	E	F	G	H	I
J	K	L	M	N	O	P	Q	R
S	T	U	V	W	X	Y	Z	

H	I	L	A	R	Y	A	N	N	D	U	F	F
8	9	3	1	9	7	1	5	5	4	3	6	6

Then we added all the numbers in Hilary's name together and got a total of 67. But we weren't finished yet. To find a category between one and nine, you need to get the numbers down to a single digit. So, we added the 6 and 7 together and got 13. But we still weren't finished. We had to add the 1 and the 3 together to make a 4.

Okay, so now we know Hilary's a four. But what does that say about her? Well, for starters, fours take duty and responsibility very seriously. Hilary's a true four—she always knows her lines, and she's never late for work. Like most fours she doesn't have a diva bone in her body. Fours can be witty and entertaining and incredibly loyal pals. But they need to watch their annoying little habit of saying exactly what's on their minds (sort of like the animated Lizzie

McGuire!). Fours get along with twos, threes, and eights.

Now figure out your own numerology. Add up the letters in your name, and see if you and Hil have anything in common, and whether you're destined to be lifelong buds.

According to numerology, **ones** are natural born leaders. They're extremely well-organized and tend to like to do all of the work by themselves. Ones love the spotlight, but they do have to learn to step aside and share the glory. Ones get along very well with twos and sixes.

Twos are more quiet and reserved. They're fair and look to understand both sides of a situation. These good friends have long memories and adore talking over old times. Twos can be supersensitive, and they need to learn to stand up for themselves in tough situations. Twos get along with sevens, eights, and other twos.

Threes are dynamic, but rarely domineering. Still, they like having things done their way and will fight to get it. Threes feel comfortable in just about any situation. They're fun to be around, but they have sharp tongues which can sometimes sting. Threes are good buds with fours and fives.

If your name makes you a **four**, you share a lot of personality traits with Hilary—how cool is that?

A **five's** restlessness will forever keep her on the go. Fives love action, adventure, and nonstop excitement. They're the life of the party. Fives also love to talk, which makes them a natural for the field of communication. But fives need to watch out—when they get a job, they tend to let their salaries slip through their fingers. Fives are the big spenders of the numerology world. Fives get along with threes, sevens, and twos.

People who are **sixes** spend a lot of their time worrying about other people's troubles. It's hard not to love a six. They're so kind, even-tempered and willing to help. But sixes can be too trusting, and wind up being taken advantage of. They need to develop a little more backbone. Sixes should spend time hanging out with ones, eights, and nines.

Sevens are trendsetters! They're full of new and exciting ideas. They're also deep thinkers who love to delve into a subject. But a seven never seems to feel she's done enough research or that her homework is complete. Nobody sets higher standards for themselves than a seven. Sevens should lighten up and hang out with their soul mates—nines, fours, other sevens, and eights.

Eights are incredibly self-disciplined people with high powers of concentration. They're born leaders who put a lot of energy into good causes. They never forget a kindness—but they rarely forget a wrong-doing either. Eights tend to hold grudges, so they need to learn forgiveness. Eights get along well with any other numbers, especially twos, fours, sixes, sevens, and nines.

Nines are humanitarians—the first ones in line to save the whales, the trees, the owls, or anything else that could be in trouble. Nines are likely to use their money and endless stamina to save the world. When it comes to a nine's emotions, she's very mercurial—up one minute and down the next. Nines need to pair off with fours, sevens, and eights.

13. | Words to Live By

Hilary Duff is well aware that she's become a role model for a lot of kids, and she takes that responsibility very seriously. She's careful not to pick movie or TV roles that show her in a bad light, or to record music that could badly influence some of her younger fans. And while you might catch Hil in some pretty funky duds, don't be looking for her to be strutting around in a string bikini in her videos anytime soon. That's *so* not her.

Meet Hilary just once, and you'll know right away that she's no Hollywood phony. She's just as she appears to be—happy, kind, giggly, and unbelievably friendly, (although she's also a little shy in public— nothing terrifies her more than public speaking). Unlike some superstars who are surrounded by bodyguards whose job it is to shoo off fans, Hilary shuns the guards and is quick to give autographs. In fact, at autograph sessions she's been known to stay far longer than she's scheduled to, just to sign for everyone. She feels really bad when she can't. As she told her fans who visited her Web site, "I want to thank everyone who came to my autograph signing . . . My manager pushed back our next appointment by forty-five minutes, but I still wasn't able to meet everybody. It always breaks my heart to leave when there are people waiting on line."

Even when she's not working, Hilary will always take the time to stop and chat with her fans. "The fans of the show are very respectful," she told a chat room audience. "And I love to meet as many as I can."

Hilary's fans are always filled with questions for her. They want to know her opinions on everything from current events to how she keeps her hair so drop dead gorgeous. Hilary's happy to share her thoughts on any subject. In fact, here's some of her best advice:

What's your advice to other teens who want to pursue a career in acting?

"Believe in yourself and follow your dreams, because you can do anything. Anything is possible if you believe in it."

How can fans get their hair to look as fab as yours?

"My hair takes a beating, so I condition a lot and use good products like Pantene and Biolage . . . and Kerastase when I swim."

What makeup (besides your own line) do you use?

"Anyone who knows me knows I'm a makeup junkie. Stila, MAC, and Hard Candy are my favorites."

Is it okay to ask a guy out on a date?

"It's hard for me sometimes. But I find that if I make the first effort instead of waiting for someone else, it works out."

Do you get along better with girls or guys?

"Guys are easier to be friends with because they don't get petty or jealous. I have a couple of close girlfriends, but sometimes it's hard. I wish girls could be each other's best friends."

What is your ideal date?

"I don't like to go out one on one unless I feel really comfortable with the person. If we go out in a group, we go to the movies, to dinner. Most of my friends drive, so sometimes we can go to Sunset Strip . . . but not for the clubs. There's a couple of under-age clubs we like to go to and dance and stuff. We don't have to worry about alcohol or drugs going on, so it's fun."

Do you think college is really necessary?

"I think college is really important, and I like school, but I don't know if I'm going to go right away. If I'm busy, there's always time for me to go later. But it's definitely important."

How did you feel when Elizabeth Smart came home safe?

"I was so happy when I heard the news that she was alive and back with her family. That shows that all the faith and prayers do help. I think we all have to be careful about strangers—when you're in public and even when you're home."

What motto do you think people should live by?

"My mom always tells me to celebrate everyone's uniqueness. I like the way that sounds."

| Fifty Fast Facts

Get your fill of Duff Stuff!

1. Full name: Hilary Ann Duff
2. Nicknames: Hil, Juicy
3. Birthday: September 28, 1987
4. Birthplace: Houston, Texas
5. Current Home: Los Angeles, California
6. Eye color: hazel
7. Height: 5'4"
8. Hair color: blond
9. Zodiac sign: Libra
10. Parents: Susan and Bob Duff
11. Sibs: one older sister Haylie (who just happens to be Hilary's role model)
12. Pets: a border collie named Remington and a

fox terrier-Chihuahua mix named Little Dog

13. Fave colors: blue, red, yellow
14. Fave lip gloss: Stila Lip Shines and MAC lip gloss
15. Fave shopping stops: Limited Too, Gap, Rampage, Bloomingdale's Juicy Couture, XOXO, Nicole Miller, and Bebe
16. Car Hil would most like to own: Mercedes CLK230
17. Fave subjects: math, world history
18. Fave Desserts: chocolate cake, chocolate cookies, ice cream
19. Fave Food: okra
20. Fave TV shows: *Smallville, Seventh Heaven, Gilmore Girls*
21. Fave gift from her friends: "I love it when my friends compile tapes for me or give me coupon books they make of special things we can do together."
22. Fave fan gifts: a sunflower, which she now keeps on her bulletin board, a handmade ring created from a nail, and beaded bracelets
23. Hilary could never live without: her cell phone, lip gloss, and moisturizer
24. Fave charities: Kids with a Cause (a charity that has celebrity spokespeople and raises money to provide underprivileged kids with arts programs,

educational opportunities, and healthcare), Disney Adventures All-Star Program (a program that encourages kids to volunteer in their own communities), Audrey Hepburn Child Benefit Fund (a charity founded in 1994 by the children of the late actress. Audrey Hepburn was very involved with helping children. This fund is a children's charity that is supported primarily by children. It's kids helping kids.).

25. Jewelry she won't leave the house without: her Tiffany heart necklace and bracelet

26. Nail polish obsession: anything by O.P.I.

27. Hilary shampoos with Biolage and Pantene products.

28. Hil is right-handed.

29. Hil loves doing photo shoots.

30. Idea of a perfect afternoon: hanging with friends and swimming

31. All time fave Christmas present: a pink Barbie Corvette

32. Dream vacay spot: Hawaii

33. Hilary likes her pizza with cheese only.

34. Hilary keeps lip gloss in the pencil holder of her locker organizer.

35. Hilary's pet peeve is cliques.

36. Hil hates it when people call her a tomboy. "I love my makeup! I'm not a tomboy!" she insists.

37. All-time idol (besides her big sis): the late Princess Diana. Hilary told a chat audience that, "I really admired Princess Diana for her charity work. It must have been amazing to travel the world and have such an impact on people's lives.

38. What makes Hil nervous: public speaking

39. If Hilary could trade places with someone for one day she'd be her special pet, Lil' Dog. "She totally has the life," Hil told *Girls' Life*. "Her day consists of lying around sleeping, sunning, and being pampered. I could deal with that!"

40. Guest stars Hilary would have most liked to have worked with on *Lizzie McGuire*: Drew Barrymore, Julia Roberts, Susan Sarandon

41. The most extravagant thing Hilary has bought for herself was a Louis Vuitton handbag. She saved for months to buy it.

42. Hilary's dream role: She'd like to star in an action movie like *Charlie's Angels*.

43. Hilary's best friend is named Taylor. Taylor's from Texas, but the girls actually met in L.A.

44. Hil's first crush was a boy in her preschool class named Timothy.

45. Hil filmed her first commercial at seven years old.

46. Person Hilary would love to record with:

Michael Jackson. "It would be a dream come true," she admitted to a chat audience. "But I'm afraid he'd say, 'Hilary who?'"

47. Hil takes hip hop and funk dance classes to stay in shape.

48. Hilary has her own credit card—but it's just for emergencies!

49. Hilary has a pair of lucky shoes. They've got a sequin sewed on each one by *Lizzie McGuire's* exec producer. They say "Good Luck" inside. Hil wore them to the 2002 Nickelodeon Kids' Choice Awards.

50. The one thing nobody knows about Hilary Duff: She sometimes sleeps with the light on. (Okay, so now everyone knows.)

Okay, so you've seen every *Lizzie McGuire* episode at least twice. You know every word to every song Hilary's ever recorded. You were the first person in your town to see *The Lizzie McGuire Movie*, and you've burned out your DVD player by watching *Agent Cody Banks* so many times. No doubt about it, you are a self-proclaimed Hilary Duff maniac.

But how well do you really know Hilary? You're about to find out. Take this quiz. Answer the questions as well as you can. Then check the chart on pages 97–98 to see how you measure up.

The answers to all the questions appear on pages 96–97. No peeking before you've given every question your best shot.

***

1. What is the name of Hilary's first short film for VideoNow?
2. Where did Hilary first say she hoped *The Lizzie McGuire Movie* would be filmed?
   A. London B. Hawaii C. Alaska
3. How tall is Hilary?
4. Who is Remington?
5. What rock superstar appeared in a Christmas episode of *Lizzie McGuire*?
   A. Ozzy Osbourne B. Mick Jagger C. Steven Tyler
6. Which of Hilary's *Agent Cody Banks* costars once played a pal of Lizzie McGuire?
7. True or false: Hilary's big sis Haylie once dated Backstreet Boy Nick Carter.
8. Where was Hilary born?
9. *Lizzie McGuire* is filmed on the same lot as what classic old time sitcom?
10. What song does Hil sing on the *Disneymania* CD?
    A. "The Tiki, Tiki, Tiki Room" B. "Someday My Prince Will Come" C. "The Mickey Mouse Club Theme"
11. What color are Hilary's eyes?
12. True or False: Hilary once guest starred on the medical drama *ER*.
13. Hilary learned to do rifle drills for which TV film?

14. True or false: Hilary is the voice of Kim on *Kim Possible*.
15. What song did Hilary record with Lil' Romeo?
16. Which parent travels from location to location with Hilary?
17. Which game show did Hilary appear on?
    A. *Hollywood Squares* B. *Jeopardy* C. *Wheel of Fortune*
18. In what film did Hilary work with Steve Martin?
19. Name Hilary's character in *Agent Cody Banks*.
20. True or False: Hilary has a fear of public speaking.
21. In what movie did Hilary play Lila Jute?
    A. *The Soul Collector* B. *Human Nature* C. *True Women*
22. What are Hilary's parents' names?
23. What MTV show did Hilary guest host?
    A. *Punk'd* B. *Dismissed* C. *TRL*
24. True or False: Hilary loves okra.
25. Hilary won a best supporting actress Young Artist Award for which film?
26. Name Hilary's first CD.
27. Who was Hilary's date at the premiere of *The Lizzie McGuire Movie*?
28. Who plays Gordo on *Lizzie McGuire*?
29. True or false: Hilary once took ballet lessons.
30. Who is Lalaine?

31. On what CD does Hilary sing "I Can't Wait"?
32. Why did Hilary go into acting?
33. What is Lizzie McGuire's brother's name?
34. How many characters did Hilary play in *The Lizzie McGuire Movie*?
35. Who is Yani Gellman?
36. Who is Juicy?
37. Other than her own brand, what is Hil's fave brand of lip gloss?
38. True or false: Hilary has her black belt in Tae Kwon Do.
39. Who is Taylor?
40. True or false: There's a Lizzie McGuire doll.

Answers to Are You a Duff Buff?:

1. *Day in the Life of Hilary Duff*
2. B
3. 5'4"
4. Hilary's border collie
5. C
6. Frankie Muniz
7. False
8. Houston, Texas
9. *I Love Lucy*
10. A
11. Hazel
12. False. It was *Chicago Hope*.
13. *Cadet Kelly*
14. False. It's Christy Carlson Romano.
15. "Tell Me a Story (About the Night Before)"
16. Her mom
17. A
18. *Cheaper by the Dozen*
19. Natalie Connors
20. True
21. B
22. Bob and Susan
23. C
24. True
26. *Santa Claus Lane*
27. Aaron Carter

28. Adam Lamberg
29. True
30. The actress who played Miranda in *Lizzie McGuire*
31. The *Lizzie McGuire* soundtrack
32. To be like her sister
33. Matt
34. Two: Lizzie and Isabella
35. The actor who played Paulo in *The Lizzie McGuire Movie*
36. Hilary (it's her nickname)
37. MAC
38. False
39. Hilary's best friend
40. True. Hilary was reported to be fascinated with the doll-making process and really pleased with the doll's likeness of her. As she told *Entertainment Tonight*, "After work one day I went into this huge truck and stood there as they took pictures. (Later) I saw the doll, and it really looks like me!"

How do you measure up?
35-40 correct: Great score! When it comes to your knowledge of Hilary Duff, you're as big a genius as Gordo!
20-34 correct: Consider yourself a huge Hilary fan!
10-19 correct: You need to get up to snuff on all

things Duff. Why not reread this book then take the test again?

1-9 correct: Uh oh! You've been spending too much time on schoolwork or something. Forget that math test, and catch up on your *Lizzie McGuire* episodes. Then pop a few Hilary Duff DVDs into your player.

| 16. | Hilary Site-ings |

If you're like most kids, you just can't get enough Duff Stuff. Luckily, there's a place (other than this book, of course!) where you can find all the news, info and photos you crave—on the World Wide Web. There are tons of Web sites dedicated to Hil, and that means you can read about Hilary, talk to other Hilary fans, and look at lots of Hilary photos all day long. After all, the Web's open 24/7.

But before you get ready to interface with other Hilary fans, there are a few things you should think about. For starters, when you're on the Net, play it safe. Don't give out your real name, address, phone number, birthday, or any other personal info. And never—EVER—meet anyone in person that you met online.

Just a word to the wise—only Hilary's closest pals

and family know her real screen name. Don't be fooled into thinking someone you meet online is the real Hilary Duff. Hil communicates with her fans by answering their questions on her official Web site: www.hilaryduff.com

Also remember, Web sites come and go. So by the time you go online, some of these sites may have closed up shop. But don't worry, new Hilary Duff Web sites are being created all the time!

Juicy Fruit
www.hilary-duff.net

Hilary Duff Pics
Hilaryduffcorner.tripod.com/gallery/gallery.html

Hilary Duff Online Shrine
www.online-shrine.com/duff/

Hilary Connection
www.Hilary-Duff.tk/

Hilary Duff
www.2tup.com/hilary_duff

Hilary Duff Zone
www. Geocities.com./hilaryduffzone/

HilaryOnline
www.hilaryonline.tk/

Teen Stars Online
www.teensonscreen.com/hilaryd.html

Agent Cody Banks Official Web site
www.agentcodybanksmovie.com

The Lizzie McGuire Movie Web site
http://disney.go.com/disneypictures/lizzie/

Hilary Duff Filmography

1997 *True Women* (TV) . . . Uncredited role

1998 *Casper Meets Wendy* (TV) . . . Wendy

1999 *The Soul Collector* (TV) . . . Ellie

2000 *Chicago Hope* (TV) Guest appearance in an episode entitled "Cold Hearts" . . . Jessie Seldon

2001 *Lizzie McGuire* (TV series) . . . Lizzie McGuire

2001 *Human Nature* . . . Young Lila Jute

2002 *Cadet Kelly* (TV) . . . Kelly Collins

2002 *The George Lopez Show* (TV) Guest appearance in an episode entitled "Team Leader" . . . Cosmetics Salesperson

2003 *Agent Cody Banks* . . . Natalie Connors

2003 *The Lizzie McGuire Movie* . . . Lizzie McGuire

2003 *Cheaper by the Dozen* . . . Lorraine Baker

2004 *The Cinderella Story* . . . Cinderella

Hilary Duff Discography

Lizzie McGuire Soundtrack (various artists)
(release date: August 13, 2002)
"I Can't Wait"

Disneymania (various artists)
(release date: September 17, 2002)
"The Tiki, Tiki, Tiki Room"

Santa Claus Lane
(release date: October 15, 2002)
"Santa Claus Lane"
"Santa Claus Is Coming to Town"
"I Heard Santa on the Radio" (duet with Christina Milian)
"Jingle Bell Rock"
"When the Snow Comes Down in Tinseltown"
"Sleigh Ride"
"Tell Me a Story (About the Night Before)" (duet with Lil' Romeo)
"Last Christmas"
"Same Old Christmas" (duet with Haylie Duff)
"Wonderful Christmas Time"

The Lizzie McGuire Movie Soundtrack (Various Artists)
(release date: April 22, 2003)

"Why Not?"
"What Dreams Are Made Of"
"Why Not McMix"

Metamorphosis
(estimated release date: Fall 2003)

About the Author

Nancy Krulik is the author of more than 150 books for children and young adults, including the *New York Times* best-sellers *Leonardo DiCaprio: A Biography*, *Taylor Hanson: Totally Taylor!*, and *Ice Age*. Besides being an established author of children's fiction, Nancy has written biographies of many of the entertainment world's brightest stars including Frankie Muniz, TLC's late Lisa "Left Eye" Lopes, XXXciting action hero Vin Diesel, *Charlie's Angels's* Drew Barrymore, Cameron Diaz, and Lucy Liu, and *NSYNC's J.C. Chasez.

Nancy lives in Manhattan with her husband, composer Daniel Burwasser, and their two children. It was her children who first introduced Nancy to *Lizzie McGuire*, and she's been a fan ever since. In fact, the whole family gathers together each evening to laugh with Lizzie and her pals in reruns of *Lizzie McGuire*.